Carlos Pascual

THE GOLDEN BOOK OF
SEVILLE

UPDATED EDITION

BONECHI

CONTENTS

The cover, layout and artwork by the Casa Editrice Bonechi *graphic artists*
in this publication are protected by international copyright.

The photographs belong to the Bonechi Archive and were produced by
Luigi Di Giovine, Paolo Giambone, Antonio Pérez González

Translated by: Studio Comunicare, Florence

ISBN 88-7009-564-9

* * *

Plaza de San Francisco, once the scene
of capital punishments, is today
Seville's administrative centre.

INTRODUCTION

Seville, the gracious city, the quintessence of Andalusia. When one thinks of Seville, one immediately has visions of crying Virgins and suffering Christs being carried through the streets during Easter, or knights with beatiful maidens riding through the city during the April festivities. Like the greatest cities, it rose from a myth that «Hercules built it». Phoenicians, Greeks, Carthaginians and Romans conquered it or were conquered by it. The old Hispalis is the best paradigm of Andalusian history. When it was the capital of the Visigothic reign it was overthrown by the Moors in 712 and in glory it rivaled with the neighbouring Sultan Cordova. Buildings rose up after the Almohad invasion in the XII century.

A century later the Holy King Ferdinand entered the city and died there beside his sword and standard. The Christian Monarchs then set up their court over Mohammedan castles. But the city's most glorious mo-

ment was when it became the capital of two new worlds, Lope de Vega's «new Babylon» where the noble and courageous contrasted with the poor: a world of American treasures, great enterprises, religious ideals, theological dogma, art and literal principles alongside a world of beggars and tramps, the true characters of minor history.

Its political decadence was similar to the country's general apathy, which increased due to some domestic tragedies, like the terrible plague in 1649 causing the death of many famous artists. But its past splendour and glory can still be felt in the unique monumental relics and the same vitality and sparkling humanity still reign over Seville which made it not only the capital of this extensive region, which stretches over the Sierra to the sea, but also the official capital of Andalusia as the seat of its autonomous government and centre of social and political problems.

◄ *A suggestive view of the Giralda, symbol of the city.*

A general view over the massive structure of the Cathedral, the third largest church in the Christian world.

THE CATHEDRAL AND ITS BELL-TOWER

The Christians built their own temple on the site of the main Mosque. However they kept the mosque's minaret which they used as the bell-tower and the Patio de los Naranjos as an unusual cloister. A great part of Seville's spirit characterizes this inseparable symbiosis.

The **Giralda**, which was in fact a Muslem minaret but cleverly disguised by the Marian symbolism of faith depicted with its four terraces with lilies, is an outstanding symbol of Seville and is one of the most beautiful and admired towers in the world.

The minaret was erected during the Almohad period near the end of the XII century; there are two sister towers also built by the Almohades: the Hassan, in Rabat, and the Kutnbis in Marrakech. The tower, almost 100 metres high, is decorated outside with arabesques

and mullioned windows which give it a delicate touch. The work was put in the hands of the poet Arubequer Benzoar by the Emir Abu Yusuf Al Mansur. Inside the tower is a solid ramp which the Christian conqueror King Ferdinand the Saint rode over a few years later. The tower was completed with four gold-plated bronze globes but an earthquake destroyed them and they were replaced in 1568 with four Renaissance elements supporting the popular weather-cock (in fact it is a revolving weather-cock and certainly isn't an appropriate symbol of faith but in Seville...) which gave its name to the whole tower.

The Gothic style dominates the cathedral which was commenced in 1420, although later work was Renaissance. According to legend, the town council appointed

The Puerta del Perdón, to the north
side of the Cathedral, with López's
plateresque decorations.

The Gate of the Campanillas.

One of the carved portals opening on the sides of the ▶
Cathedral.

all the famous architects, sculptors and stone-masons to build the greatest temple on earth, and they almost succeded as Seville cathedral is depicted on the floor of the Vatican in Rome, as the third biggest Christian temple, only excelled by St. Peter's itself, Saint Paul's in London and by the new Abidjan cathedral. It is 130 metres long, 76 metres wide and features 68 domes supported by 40 solid pillars as well as 93 stained-glass windows which let light filter through and shine on thousands of shadowy figures and statues made of marble, clay, iron, wood, and stone and on a whole cosmic world of friezes, capitals, altarpieces, tombs and stained-glass windows.

The work on the building continued from 1502 to 1519. In 1511 the dome was destroyed and later rebuilt by Gil de Hontanón. The most famous architects who contributed were Juan Norman, Pedro de Toledo, Juan de Alava, Gil de Hontánon, (Dome) Diego de Riaño and Martin de Gainza (Sacristy of the Chalices) Juan de Meda (Royal Chapel). Some of the greatest artists expressed their talent here: Pedro de Campaña, Roelas, Herrera el Mozo, Murillo, Zurbarán, Valdés, Alejo Fernandez, Alonso Cano and Luis de Vergas. Sculptors like

Fancelli, Andrea della Robbia, Martinez Montañés, Miguel Perrin, etc. performed the terracotta decoration and marble tombs; Nufro Sanchez built the choir and Dancart achieved the choir-stalls; Arfe engraved the monstrance in silver creating «the best and oldest existing work of art in silver while Bartolomeo Morel worked in bronze; Francisco de Salamanca, Antonio de Palencia, Sancho Munoz, Juan de Yepes, Esteban and Diego Idoboro worked with wrought iron.

When you enter this immense church you enter into a world of art where every piece is worth looking at, but there are a few special items which deserve a closer look.

First of all there is the **Capilla Mayor** which houses the oldest Christian *altarpiece*, lost in a symphony of shapes and colour. It is 200 square metres in size with more than a thousand figures depicting the holy story. No less than 26 artists from different parts of the world worked on this piece, the first being a Fleming, Dancart, in 1482, followed by Bernardo and Francisco Ortega, Jorge Fernandez, etc. The central part was finished in 1521, while the work on the sides was carried out from 1550 to 1564 by Diego Vazquel, Nurfo

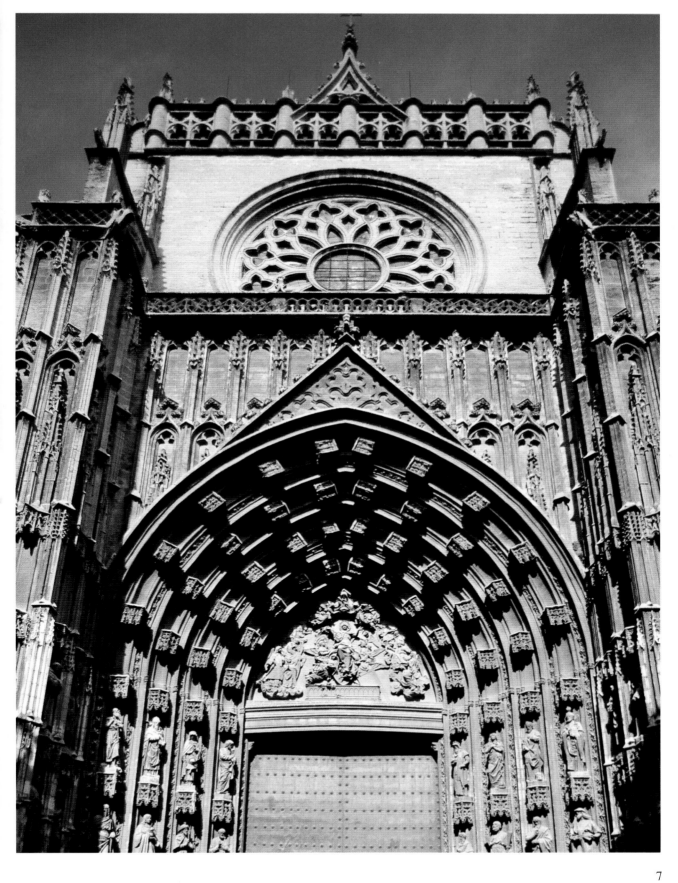

From the top of the Giralda
one can fully appreciate the cross-shaped
structure of the Cathedral.

Two additional outer views of the Cathedral ▶
and the gate called Puerta del Perdón.

The Gothic Puerta de los Palos,
with the sixteenth century sculptures
done by the Maestro Miguel.

◄ *The interior of the Cathedral with its superb ceiling in flamboyant Gothic style.*

A detail of the Nativity in the Cathedral's retablo.

11

The external part of the Royal Chapel's apse erected in plateresque style.

The altar of the Royal Chapel, with the ▶ venerated statue of the Virgen de los Reyes.

de Ortega, Juan López, Pedro de Heredia, etc. It consists of 45 paintings of the life of Christ and the Virgin Mary together with paintings of the principal Sevillian saints. This huge, illuminating cosmos of paintings, figurines and canopies are used as the background for all great ceremonies or for the graceful dance of the «six» during the public holiday of the Immaculate Conception or Corpus Christi. The dance of the «six» is a traditional Sevillian dance where the choir boys appointed to sing at religious ceremonies dress up as page-boys from the XVI century and have the privilege of dancing in front of the Arfe monstrance. They are simple ancient Span-

ish dances, like the Bolero, whose gracefulness and lightness contrast strikingly with the elaborate velvet and gold reflections inside the cathedral.

In the Museum of Arts and Popular Traditions you can follow the evolution of the costumes and traditions of the Sevillian «six».

The magnificent railings which enclose the main chapel and which seem to reflect the multi-coloured altarpiece with its «Plateresque style», are by Francisco de Salamanca and Sancho Muñoz who together carried out the work from 1518 to 1533.

Behind the main chapel stands the Renaissance

The Sacristía de los Cálices
in flamboyant Gothic style features
on its altar a beautiful Crucifix sculptured
in 1603 by Montáñes.

The plateresque Sacristia Mayor houses the large
Renaissance ostensory in silver by Juan de Arfe
weighing 300 kilograms.

At the head of the Cathedral's transept, four heralds ▶
representing the kingdoms of Castile, León, Aragon,
and Navarre support the sarcophagus containing the
presumed mortal remains of Christopher Columbus.

Capilla Real, built at the beginning of 1551 by Martin de Gainza who was succeded by Hernan Ruiz; it was then completed by Juan de Maeda in 1575. The chapel conceived as a Royal Pantheon houses the tombs of two of Sevillian's most famous figures. The first is *Alfonso X the Wise*, who, encouraged by his mother Beatrix of Swabia, proceeded to reign unsuccessfully in the Sevillian castles; a dream which came true many years later for Charles V; the tomb of his mother lies opposite.

In the centre, in front of the high altar, stands a rich XVIII century silver arch, a gift from Philip V which guards the tomb of another great Sevillian figure, the Holy King Ferdinand III; he conquered the Saracen power and is the city's patron saint: «the loyalest, truest, noblest, most honest and humble king» according to the epigraph written in Latin, Muslem, Hebrew and Spanish.

The two XVI century sacristies, the **Sacristia Mayor** and **Sacristia de los Calices** are both authentic museums within the cathedral. Amidst the opulent setting of the Sacristia Mayor we can admire the Silver Montrance by Juan de Arfe and the so-called «tablas alfonsinas», a *triptych shrine* and gift from Alfonso X. The treasure honours its name with numerous chalices, shrines and religious offerings. Mention must be made of *Goya's paintings*, depicting the Sevillian saints, Justa and Rufina, the popular «cacharreras». Paintings by Murillo, Morales (*Pietà*), Valdes Leal, Tritan etc. A moving *crucifix* by Martinez Montañés presides over this small art gallery which one comes across before leaving the cathedral. Our curiosity will be aroused by a pompous collection of sculptures which are one of the latest additions to the temple's treasures. We are referring to the romantic tomb of **Christopher Columbus**, by Arturo Melida. It was brought here in 1899 from the Habana cathedral and is only a symbolic tomb as it is empty.

A typical statue of Christopher stands behind it, a statue easily found in other cathedrals as according to tradition, whoever looks at Saint Christopher is guaranteed the following 24 hours of life. If we look up at the domes we can see some XIX century stained-glass windows together with more valuable ones executed in the XVI century by Flemish artists.

A panoramic view of the city from the Giralda.

A view of the Giralda.

The Giralda at night. ►

On the following pages: the city and the Plaza de la Virgen de los Reyes seen from the top of the Giralda, and the huge mass of the tower.

Two views of the Patio de los Naranjos (the courtyard of the almohade mosque). It is planted with orange trees and centered by a cup-shaped fountain — a charming spot dominated by the Cathedral's Gothic façade.

PATIO DE LOS NARANJOS

The **Patio de los Naranjos** is the only cloister in the cathedral. It was once the patio of an ancient mosque and is mentioned in all the best-loved clichés about the city. The scent of the orange-blossom in the spring air seems to mingle with the murmuring of the beggars and the cripples who used to sit on the steps outside and even today we still find them waiting for tourists.

There is a fountain in the middle which comes from a Visigothic cathedral. A curious object is found beside the Lagarto door, through an original Mosque arch; it is a wooden crocodile hanging from the roof which gave rise to well-known legends of princesses and dragons; however, it is seemingly a saurian replica which was sent to Alfonso X by the Sultan of Egypt in 1260, at a time when such a reptile was considered a monster in these parts.

From the Giralda, a view over the Alcazar's battlemented walls and towers.

The Puerta del Léon, which opens in the circuit of walls, is crowned by an azulejo with a rampant lion. ▶

LOS REALES ALCAZARES

Despite the Arab influence which reigns in these palaces, little in fact remains of the first Moresque constructions. Only the wall around the castle is still standing, containing the **Puerta del León** on the entrance to the Alcazar dating back to the XII century. The enclosure continues right up to the river with the Torre de Abdelaziz, the Torre de la Plata, and the **Torre del Oro** which faced another sister tower on the other side of the riverbed, hence forming a barrier to prevent enemy ships from entering. The **Patio del Yeso** also forms part of the early structure and is a unique example of Almohad architecture in Spain.

But fires, earthquakes, reforms and later extensions either wiped out or absorbed these early structures. What we see now is the castle of King Peter, one of the most complete examples of Mudejar art, that is to say, a Christian palace finished by Islamic or Christian craftsmen with a Muslem artistic training. The castle of King Peter I of Castile, nick-named the Cruel King, was completed in the XIV century; later, extensions and alterations were made and unfortunately badly-planned Romantic restorations were carried out. The Catholic Monarchs appointed Moorish craftsmen to work on it. Then, in 1526, to celebrate Charles V wedding, it underwent some extensions and further modernizations were carried out under Philip V in 1624. All in all, it is still one of the best examples of Mudejar art, this unusual Spanish style which was formed on Christian soil from an Islamic and Jewish tradition during a transitional era when Christian intolerance hadn't yet ruined the co-existence of Christian, Islamic and Jewish cultures.

The Mudejar art here is over-loaded with colour and imagination and lies on the border-line of the sublime and Kitsch, typical of the oldest cliché of Andalusian «bad taste» and Spanish traditionalism. José Péman amusingly points out that «King Peter» was an Andalusian type «orientalist» which anticipated the orientalism of Zorrilla or of Villaespesa, imitating the style of Baghdad.

It wouldn't be right to generalize too much on Andalusian constructions by calling the Palace or the Alhambra Arabic or by ignoring the strong Roman influence in Cordova, like the Roman columns found in the Mosque.

The Patio de la Montería, whose name originates from that of the royal guard, the Monteros de Espinosa.

After walking through the Puerta del Léon, we find the Patio de la Monteria which dates back to the times of Mexuar and which separates the palace from the city; we then reach the Patio del Leon where we can admire the main façade of the palace, erected in 1364 and whose wings were later enlarged in the XVI and XVII centuries. On the second part of this façade a Cufic inscription praising Allah is engraved next to the Gothic inscription in memory of the creator of the work.

The **Patio de las Doncellas**, surrounded by lobe-shaped arches, forms the central nucleus of the residence. On the walls there are delicately engraved plasterwork and XVI enamel tile panels which are the best examples of Mudejar art.

The Patio de las Doncellas is characterized by a rich decoration of azulejos, dating back to the 16th century and undoubtedly the most beautiful in the entire palace, and by multi-coloured lacunar ceilings.

The soft and delicate finishing touch is accentuated by the colourful panelling and doors. Following Arabic tradition, all public and ceremonial activities took place here, while the private life evolved around the Patio de las Muñecas; the names of the rooms are arbitary and originate from traditional everyday life.

The rooms which surround the Patio de las Doncellas are more official in character. They consist of the Charles V «Salón del techo», named after the lavish Renaissance cedar-wood lacunar ceiling; three small rooms of Maria de Padilla and the main room, which is also the most beatiful in the castle, the **Salón de Embajadores**. In the front archway, the repetitive Nazarene inscription «Only God is victorious» is engraved in Arabic. The doors were carved by Toledan craftsmen. Apart from the dome, the rest of the decoration is of the King Peter period; it was carried out in the XV century and later restored. There is a surprising series of portraits of all the Spanish kings up to Philip III with their coats-of-arms and dates of their reigns, set in Gothic arches. The room at the end is the dining-room with Philip II period panelling.

The **Patio de las Muñecas**, the centre of the private quarters, is elegant. The columns date back to the Caliph period and come from the then-devastated Cordovan Medina Zahara (the stuccoes of the upper part were re-made in 1843).

After climbing up a Charles V period staircase with

*Two views of the Patio de las Doncellas.
The arches over the colonnade
are decorated with lobe tracery.*

The Salón de Embajadores with handsome
mudéjar decorations, and its high dome
dressed with gilded stalactite work.

Following pages: the Salón de Embajadores
dates from the period of Peter I, and is among
the most beautiful rooms of the Alcazar.

beautiful XVI century enamel tiles, we reach a series of
rooms decorated with Flemish, French and Spanish
XVII and XVIII century tapestries. In the **Oratorio de
los Reyes Católicos** there are more tiles which form a
small altar, painted by Niculoso Pisano in 1504. Next
we come to the Salas de los Infantes de Reyes, King
Peter's bedroom and that of Doña Maria with more panelling and enamel tiles.

From the Patio del León we reach the **Salas de los
almirantes** which houses the Casa de la Contratación;
it is where some of the most important voyages to the
new world, like Magellan's trip round the world, were
planned. The walls are covered with XVII and XVIII
tapestries, and in the famous painting «*la Virgen de los
navagantes*» by Alejo Fernandez, many people claim to

have seen the effigy of Colombus on the right, surrounded by the Pinzón brothers.

From the Patio del León we also reach the Patio de
Maria de Padilla, which stands among a series of structures built during the XVIII century, during Philip V's
reign, over the ruins of a Gothic palace dating back to
either the end of the XIII or the beginning of the XIV
century with only a few half-buried traces left, like the
arcade known as the Baños de Maria de Padilla. The
Gothic chapel, a wide room which was made into an
oratory by Philip V, and a Charles V room are to be
found among these Gothic buildings.

In the chapel, there are XVI century enamel tiles and
a XVIII century Baroque altarpiece. The splendid *Nativity* from the Granada School stands out in the collec-

29

tion of paintings. In Charles V's room, with a roof made of ogival domes and tiles painted by Cristobál de Augusta in 1577, there is a splendid tapestry collection in bright colours depicting the adventures of the emperor during the conquest of Tunis.

The Arab-Andalusian tradition of having an important and complementary place inside the court residences gave rise to the **Jardínes del Alcazar**. They were later changed by successive residents.

Charles V added a *Pavilion* with galleries of columns and beautiful enamel tiles by Juan Hernández (1543), dominating the section named after the king. Avenues lined with palm-trees and geometric box-wood

Preceding pages:
two views of the Patio de las Muñecas.

The dormitory de los Reyes Moros. ▶

The Patio de las Muñecas or Patio of the Dolls is thus named owing to the female heads on the capitals.

In the Cuarto del Almirante, the retablo of the Madonna of the sailors is kept; the figure to the right at the Virgin's feet is a portrait of Columbus.

The gardens of Catalina de Ribera near the east wall of the Alcazar, laid out in terraces and planted with palms and exotic trees, are among Andalusia's noblest artistic expressions.

The statue of the Immaculate Conception ▶ on the Plaza del Triunfo.

paths which widen out to protect a spring on ground level or a fountain here and there form a picture of classic Renaissance peacefulness. Then the neo-classic *Los Grutescos* were placed there. The large pond, which reflects the tops of the palm-trees, features a *bronze fountain* of Mercury by Diego Pesquera. The pied-à-terre, a large room with marble columns, leads onto the Patio de Banderas; from there we can reach the Plaza del Triunfo, outside the enclosure, whose name brings to mind images of horse-driven carriages parked at this point. There are all types of gardens from the Arab period right up to the present day. But, however different they may be, they are all characterized by the same Andalusian spirit filled with the sweet, light perfume of the orange and lemon blossoms and jazmine flowers, and the soft trickling of the water from the springs and fountains which reflects the colourful glazes of the tiles.

SEVILLE, THE NEW BABYLON

Spain's Golden Age, with the political unification of the country and discovery of the new land filling it with the soldiers, missionaries, saints, theologians and beggars was also the golden age for Seville. Lope de Vega who dedicated some of his talents to her, called the city the «New Babylon». The fact that the Guadalquivir was still navigable and the city had a port explains its sudden boom.

As a result of this change, Seville was overcome with many types of palaces, convents, churches, monuments and houses which are still standing today. To complete this picture of the city, it is worth mentioning some of the best known structures.

*Casa Lonja, with its severe architecture,
contains the Archives of the Indies - a valuable
source of information on the
Spanish colonization of America.*

CASA LONJA

The **Plaza del Triunfo** lies between the cathedral and the castle's walls and houses a pretentious monument in memory of the Sevillian theologians who explained the *Immaculate Conception* of the Virgin Mary hence earning the official Marian title: the **Casa Lonja** which rises up admist the palm-trees, and houses the **Archive of India**, built by Herrera between 1583 and 1598 to be used as the Exchange or Casa de Contratación to deal with business with the West Indies. But the Archive remained there when it was set up in 1784. All the documents regarding the discovery of America, conquests, and later discoveries are kept here for reference for experts and researchers.

THE TOWN HALL

The Town hall stands on the opposite side of the Cathedral, dominating both the Plaza Nueva and de San Francisco where the famous and most lively Calle Sierpes begins, filled with classical Cervantine rendez-vous. It was built in 1527 according to designs by Diego de Riano and is a fundamental example of «Plateresque» art, Renaissance art with rich decorations formed by the delicate gold and silver work of its craftsmen. Besides its interesting architecture, it also contains some first class paintings and artistic objects.

HOSPITAL DE LA CARIDAD

The Hospital de la Caridad was founded in the XVI century as the seat of an Association whose pious tasks were to comfort prisoners sentenced to death just before they were executed and to give the executed a Christian burial. Its founder was Don Miguel de Manara, a cocky young Sevillian gentleman who finally repented and converted to charity to redeem his past. His character also inspired the famous universal mythical figure of Don Juan Tenorio referred to by writers and musicians like Tirso de Molina, Zorrilla, Molière, Mozart, Max Frisch, Maranon, etc.

The majolica-tiled façade of the church of San Jorge, in the Hospital de la Caridad.

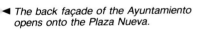 The back façade of the Ayuntamiento opens onto the Plaza Nueva.

The Triumph of Death, a traditional theme in Spanish paintings.

CASA DE PILATOS

The Casa de Pilatos owned by the Dukes of Medinaceli, is one of the most luxurious mansions in Seville, due to its architectural wealth and art collections. Built at the end of the XV century, it combines the Mudejar, Renaissance and Gothic styles. According to legend, it is thus named as it is a true reproduction of the palace of Pontius Pilate in Jerusalem. Rooms, which have been converted into an interesting museum of classic statuary, open up onto the main patio, with the best example of Spanish enamel tiles.

Casa de Pilatos, with a double order of 24 arches and extremely fine embossed azulejo decorations.

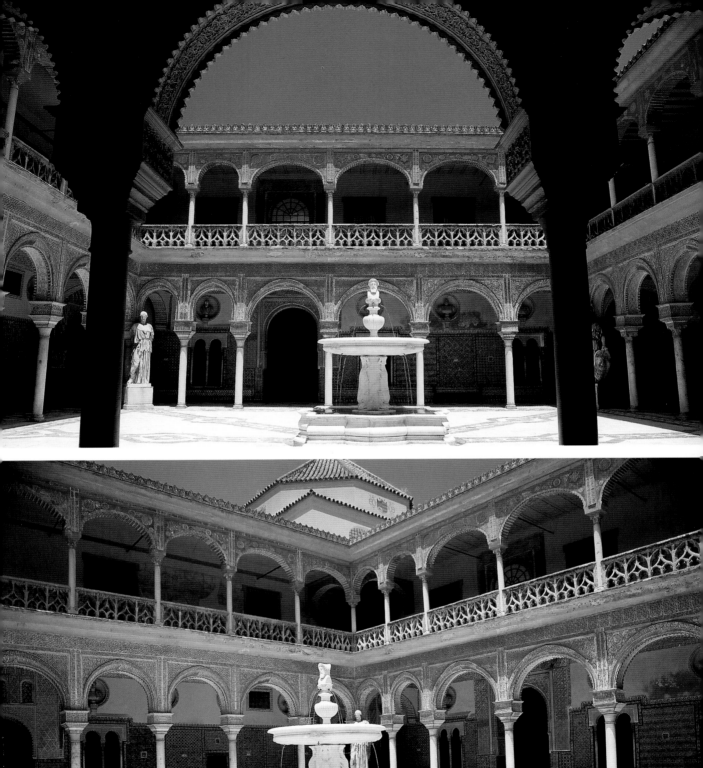

*The eighteenth century
Puerta de la Macarena, near to the
homonymous basilica.*

THE GRACIOUS CITY

There is no other city in Spain, or in the world according to some Sevillians, as gracious as Seville; the omnipresence of happiness, openness, good humour, imagination and love of life which dominates every gesture, saying and corner of the city, make it unique.

We obviously can't «visit» their gestures and sayings but we can feel them immediately as soon as we enter the city. The true graceful character is reflected in the street corners which are crammed together forming their own districts and well worth visiting.

The most famous quarter in the world is undoubtedly the *Barrio de Santa Cruz*, a small maze hidden between the castle walls and the Murillo gardens. A fantastic world with its evocative street names like Callejón del Agua, Calle de la Pimienta, Vida, Jamerdana, Mezquita, Cruces etc. In the *Plaza de Santa Cruz* there is a XVIII

century wrought iron cross and it reminds us of the folklore tradition of the «cruces de mayo» or May crosses. In every street there are balconies adorned with flowers, garden walls covered with jazmines and doorways filled with flowers and fountains. It isn't a typical ancient Moorish quarter as one might think; in fact the «barrio» was «invented» in the XX century by the most famous Spanish expert on tourism, the Marquis de la Vega Inclán, who also invented the Toledan Casa del Greco and other things of the same style.

Another world famous district is the **Triana barrio**. Rodrigo de Triana was the first man to catch sight of the New Land, and later many things and people were named after him, for example the river bank of Seville when the river was still navigable as well as bull fighters, dancers, etc. Although nowadays it has lost its

The Barrio de Santa Cruz,
with its whitewashed houses.

The Cruz de Cerranjeria dating back
to 1695, with its elaborate
wrought-iron volutes.

Following page:
The venerated statue of the Virgen de Macarena,
attributed to the sculptress Luisa Roldàn.

original physical and urbanistic form, it hasn't lost its
spiritual identity. The Trianeros are proud of belonging
to Triano and when they carry their Virgin, Esperanza
de Triana, they fight, if necessary, with the people from
the enemy district who are devoted to the «Macarena»,
the rival Virgin who characterizes and animates the
whole area with its pure Sevillian Basilica, which stands
in front of a triumphal doorway, and is overcome by
mystery and movement at midnight on Holy Thursday.

Previous page:
The Hospital de Venerables Sacerdotes houses
the Museo de las Cofradias, where models and
"pasos" belonging to the Hermandades
of Seville and the small cities of the province
and used in the Holy Week Procession, are on exhibit.

On this page: Scenes from the lively Barrio de Santa
Cruz with its typical restaurants, taverns, and
courtyards in the plazas de Alfaro, de la Alianza,
de Doña Elvira, and de Callejon del Agua.

Four pictures of the fascinating,
mysterious Barrio de Santa Cruz.

Portal and balcony of the San Telmo
palace's main façade once the
residence of the dukes of Montpensier.

*Two views of the Parque de Maria Luisa
with its lush vegetation and romantic corners.
The "gloriette" of Gustavo Adolfo Bécquer
and the statue of the poet are by the Sevillian
sculptor Coullat Valera.*

PARQUE DE MARIA LUISA

The parks and gardens scattered around the city form the framework of this picture. There are ancestral gardens, like the castle's gardens, municipal ones like the Murillo garden, or noble gardens like the famous Parque de Maria Luisa. A romantic park used as a setting for sweet Spanish melodies and whose avenues are named after the Swans or the most important Romantic poet of Spain, the Sevillian Gustavo Adolfo Bécquer. Summerhouses, pathways, horse-driven carriages, pools filled with water lilies and labyrinths of enamel tiles all form a perfectly romantic setting.

On this and the following pages: several views
of the Plaza de España with the impressive
1929 Spanish-American Exposition buildings.
Benches are handsomely dressed with ceramic panels
illustrating allegories relating
to Spain's 58 provinceses.

PLAZA DE ESPAÑA

Pavilions for the great Hispo-American Fair were set
up here in 1929. And what could have in fact been the
park's downfall, turned out to be its crowning glory.
Permanent structures were built for the occasion, like
the **Plaza de España** which was created with traditional
materials (fashionable tiles, enamel tiles, imagination,
colour) and which now plays an important role in the
scenario of Seville.

The destiny of the Parque de Maria Luisa is definitely
linked to the theme of America. Apart from holding the
Hispo-American Exhibition there and naming its streets

The façade of the Archaeological Museum, rich in works of art.

In the Plaza de América stands the pavilion that houses the interesting Museo de Artes y Costumbres Populares.

The façade of the Museo de Artes y Costumbres Populares, and below, the Plaza de América with doves in flight. ►

and avenues after heroes of the Latin-American era, its other great square is in fact called the **Plaza de America**. An oval area surrounded by gardens, terraces and doves, now strongly connected to Andalusia. In fact one of the three pavilions which stands at one of the ends, is the **Pabellón Real**. The other two pavilions opposite are more interesting for tourists: the Pabellón Renacimiento, on the south side, houses the **Archaeological Museum of Seville**, one of the most interesting museums in the country for its statuary and Roman antiques as Andalusia was one of the most romanized provinces of the Empire. There are also pre-Roman exhibits, like the Carambolo Treasure which dates back to the native civilisation of the «Turdetanos».

The north pavilion is called the «Pabellón Mudéjar» and houses the **Museum of Art and Popular Customs**.

Above the Paseo de Cristóbal Colón rises the Golden Tower, thus named because it was once covered in gilded azulejos.

A nocturnal view of the Calle Betis on the banks of the Guadalquivir.

The buildings of the Real Maestranza: the Plaza de Toros and one of the inner chapels.

PLAZA DE TOROS

A visit is necessary to find out about traditional ways of life in Seville. There is a vast collection of pieces of furniture, household objects, ceramics, clothes, jewels games, bullfighting articles, etc.

On the subject of bullfighting, mention must be made of the most beautiful and well-known bull ring in the world, the **Real Plaza de la Maestranza**. It was built in 1760, and touched up later, with lavish stone and tiles resting on marble columns, where the most famous bull fighters such as Joselito and Belmonte risked death.

A few kilometres from Seville, one comes across
the Roman ruins of Itálica, the town founded
by the Scipiones and the birthplace
of the Emperor Trajan, Hadrian and Theodosius.

RUINAS DE ITALICA

Another interesting archaeological spot outside Seville, is the Ruinas de Italica. They are the remains of a
Roman city which over the centuries was used as a
quarry to build mosques, palaces, convents; in the XVI
century, the poet Rodrigo Caro described them as being
«fields of solitude and despair».

However, you can trace the line of the roads and
pavements, the form of the villas with their mosaic
floors, the drainage system and urbanisation structures,
and the remains of the amphitheatre which gives us an
idea of the importance of the city. Next to it stands the
Monasterio de S. Isidoro which was built with the
same stone by Guzmán el Bueno, one of the national
heroes who threw down his dagger used to sacrifice his
son from the battlements of the fortress rather than
handing it over to the Unfaithful in exchange. His body
rests there in the shadow of a beautiful altarpiece by
Martinez Montañés.

Examples of antique Roman statuary
in the museum and in the Italic amphitheatre.

On the following page: a night view of
the bridge known as La Barqueta.